MelBay Presents

Kyle Creed
Clawhammer
Banjo Master

Clawhammer Banjo Tablature as Played by Kyle with modern interpretations by Bob Carlin and Dan Levenson

CD Contents

1 2 3 4 5 6 7 8 9 0

Visit us on the Web at www.melbay.com — E-mail us at email@melbay.com

Acknowledgements

From Bob

Thanks particularly to Tom Mylet, who began the process with Kyle of tabbing out Creed's banjo style, made the recordings that served as the cornerstone of this book and who put me on the path toward appreciating Kyle's banjo playing.

Thanks also to the Southern Folklife Collection at the University of North Carolina-Chapel Hill for dubs of Tom Carter and Blanton Owen's field tapes of Kyle Creed and the late Ray Alden/Field Recorders Collective, Bobby Patterson/Heritage Records and Charlie Faurot/County Records for issuing Creed's banjo playing.

Kyle's daughters Lenora and Ida Lou allowed us to reprint family photos and supported this project from the beginning. Ken Landreth shot photographs at the Kyle Creed Banjo Show and gave us permission to use some of them here. *Banjo NewsLetter* printed my early attempts at teaching Kyle's banjo style, which led to this book.

And thanks to Dan, my coauthor, who helped to make this idea a reality.

From Dan

To the many folks who have kept this music alive over the years
as well as those who continue to do so.

To my wife, The Lovely Miss Jennifer for continuing to support me in my
chosen path.

To Bob Carlin, my coauthor. He is one of my earliest inspirations and now peer and friend.

Special thanks also goes to Audio Technica for providing the AT 2020 USB microphone used in the recording of my tracks for this book.

And, as always, to The Mel Bay family and company who provide us an outlet for our work.

Photo of 1733 Kyle Creed built banjo courtesy of Kevin Fore.

Kyle Creed photo courtesy of the Kyle Creed family.

Table of Contents

All tunes are traditional and/or in the public domain.

Tablature has been set with makemusic - Coda Music's *finale*® software.

All arrangements © 2010 by Dan N. Levenson and Bob Carlin

Introductory Notes About the Book

Welcome to *Kyle Creed: Clawhammer Banjo Master*. This is the first in what we intend to be a series of transcriptions of tunes from the old masters who gave definition to our style of old time clawhammer banjo playing. Upcoming masters visited in this series will include some of our favorite banjo players such as Wade Ward and Fred Cockerham. These players have since passed on but not before sharing their music with the few dedicated people who traveled to meet them in the earlier days of old time music. It is through their generosity that we have this beautiful music to pass on to you and for you to pass on to the next generation of players in order to keep this tradition alive.

Please note, this book is not intended to be an instructional book. Should you find you need an instructional book, please get Dan's *Clawhammer Banjo From Scratch* (Mel Bay 20190 BCD) and the corresponding DVD's (Mel Bay 5003 DVD) which are also available from Mel Bay.

Also, in order to better understand the style of music being presented here, you will find Bob's *Carolina Clawhammer* DVD series (Mel Bay–CT 106 & 107) a helpful reference for the playing style of the region and the players represented by it.

About Written Music - Written music has many limits when it comes to accurately representing true music. There are many subtleties and inflections that cannot be represented by the limited pallet that written music provides. Also, in one written pass through any tune, there may be countless variations of notes and techniques that would not ALL be played in one playing of the tune. This is done so you have as many options as possible to chose from when you play the tune. Learn the written music, but listen recorded versions, too. If you listen long enough, you will find that you can sing the tune before you ever try to play it. Which brings me to:

Creativity - Beyond The Right (Write) way - There is no doubt these versions will not be the only version you come upon as you journey through the old time music world; nor will these be the ones you always want to play or hear. These tabs are intended to be a starting point, not the ending. In reality, there is no one right way to play any tune. Everything is open to your interpretation. If there is a right way it is the way you like it. HOWEVER, if you are interested in an historic interpretation of these tunes and their development since being brought into the common repertoire from a respected source, these transcriptions will get you well on your way.

About the CD

The CD accompanying this book is presented to give you a recorded example of the banjo tabs as they were written in this book. Each of us plays each tune one time through. The version of the tune you hear on the cd is intended to be close but not necessarily exactly as written. In most cases, the recorded tempos are slower than performance speed and intended to be for demonstration purposes only. Dan's tracks were recorded with an Audio Technica 2020 USB mic directly to an iMac.

About the Tunes

The tunes chosen for this volume represents the most common tunes played by Kyle Creed and you have been provided two tabs for each tune.

The first tab provide has been transcribed from Kyle's playing by Bob Carlin and accurately represents Kyle's own playing. In many instances you will find some alternate measures suggested along with the complete tab. These will help you create variations and are reflective of

the variety and richness that was associated with Kyle's playing.
The second tab was written by me and reflects more modern methods of getting Kyle's sound.
You will find some things easier here – there are very few if any *drags* or *galax licks* for instance
– but others more difficult in order to recreate the sounds you expect to hear in Kyle's playing
without some of the more common techniques he used regularly.

In all cases, these tunes should be playable by most players having good basic clawhammer
skills though you may have to add a technique or two to your *toolbox*.

Reading the Tablature

This book is written with a type of music notation known as tablature. Reading tablature is in

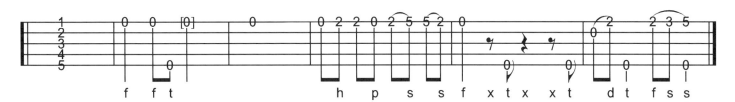

many ways easier than reading music.
In tablature the lines of the staff indicate the strings of the banjo and the notes are numbers
which tell you the fret numbers on the string. In tablature (see example), the top line of the staff
represents the first string of your banjo and the bottom line the 5th (short) string.

The second measure shows some of the notes used. A quarter note counts as 1 beat (say, "one").
Eighth notes count as 1/2 beat each so, 2 eighth notes = one quarter note (say, "one and"), and a
half note counts for 2 beats or 2 times a quarter note (say, "one, two"). The next measure shows a
whole note, which counts as 4 beats (say, "one, two, three, four").

The letters under the notes indicate whether you use the finger - "f" or the thumb - "t" of your
right hand to play the note. An "x" (5th measure) indicates silence used both for rests and
skipped beats — ie., you don't play this note but your hand keeps moving up and down even so.

The h, p and s give playing directions for your left hand. The "h" is the symbol for a hammer-on,
the "p" is the symbol for a pull-off and the "s" indicates a slide. I also use a "slur" (the curve above
the notes) for the slide.

The "d" is a new marking for us and indicates a *drag* where you are playing two consecutive
strings with the same finger over one beat by delaying or slowing down your downstroke takes a
full beat to play both notes with your fingernail. This leads us to the *Galax Lick*.

"Galax Lick" - Here you actually roll two beats with the finger and thumb where each gets a
full beat instead of the usual half beat for each. Your finger plays the first notes of the series
— either a hammer-on or slide on the first string or a *drag* of the finger across multiple strings
— followed by a continued motion as your hand comes up the thumb plays the fifth string (see
the last measure of the tab example). That puts the fifth string sounding at the beginning of a
beat instead of the end. You are actually taking 2 beats to complete the down-up hand motion of
clawhammer playing instead of the usual one beat.

Notes with no marking under them should fit the rule that if the note is on the first half of the
beat, it is played with your finger. If on the second half of the beat, it is played with your thumb.

Bob's Method

Welcome to the first clawhammer banjo tab book dedicated to the playing and repertoire of master clawhammer banjoist Kyle Creed. In my part of this book, you'll find my transcriptions of a large part of Creed's banjo tunes played the way Kyle played them. I am proud that this is the first guide to capture such intimate details of Kyle Creed's banjo style on some of the core tunes from his region.

Kyle Creed was a part of the Round Peak Three (so named for the area in northwestern North Carolina where they lived) which also includes Tommy Jarrell and Fred Cockerham. It was the recordings of these three fiddle and banjo players helped to launch the old time music revival of the 1970's & 1980's.

While techniques like playing over the fingerboard, widespread among current clawhammer banjoists, can be directly traced back to Kyle, he also played an additional role, that of a luthier. Creed's banjos have become iconic within the current old time music scene in defining how an open-back banjo should sound.

I met Kyle Creed, albeit briefly, on my first sojourn to the Southern mountains. I didn't get to hear him play on that trip. Of course, I was familiar with his music from the County Records *Clawhammer Banjo* series and the *Camp Creek Boys* LP's but, a combination of availability (Tommy Jarrell and Fred Cockerham were both retired and largely at home, but, Kyle was still working) and circumstance steered me away from Kyle Creed's playing and toward that of Tommy and Fred. In part because of that, it took many years for me to gain an understanding of Kyle's minimalist approach.

Partially directed by Kyle's student Tom Mylet, I discovered Creed's rich musical legacy mostly through field and home recordings. When I realized how under-represented Kyle was in the current wealth of instructional materials, it became obvious that I should undertake this book.

Ever since my first trip to the South in 1975, I realized the importance of learning how the traditional musicians played. One didn't have to always imitate or even keep within the confines of a *traditional* style, but, it seemed to sure help your music if you understood how the tradition worked. As long as you "knew how a banjo was played," you'd be alright. That first journey opened up a whole world of music to me, leading to my attendance of summer fiddlers' conventions and multiple visits to the homes of those musicians I admired, both young and old.

One of the obvious rules of learning directly from the older players was that it then became my job to pass that information along to someone else. It's a role that I've taken seriously. I was handed a precious object—a tune, a technique—and then asked to treat that musical object with respect. Fred Cockerham once said to "tell 'em [after he was gone] that Fred Cockerham used to could play a banjo, but, he can't anymore." It has become my duty, along with a handful of others making the same journey, to care-take the tradition for future generations and to share what makes it tick.

This book is another piece in my passing along the tradition to a new generation of players. I hope you find the information contained in this guide useful in your quest of clawhammer enlightenment. I find the more I know the more enjoyable music making becomes.

Have fun with this information and may it lead you another step in your learning process.

----Bob Carlin, Lexington, NC, November, 2009

Dan's Method

When I first began to play clawhammer banjo seriously — around 1985, I was very lucky to have both the guidance of books as well a wealth of recordings from then current as well as masters passed on. County Records had released its *Clawhammer Banjo 1, 2 and 3* lp's giving me access to sound of the older players. And, Highwoods Stringband and The Horseflies as well as performers as co-author Bob Carlin and others made hearing the *modern* versions of clawhammer readily available as well.

I had been dancing with the *Coal Country Cloggers* and shortly after that found myself working for a store that sold all of these great records and traveled to some of the best gatherings of the day as a vendor. This gave me incredible opportunities to both meet and play with some of the most influential players of the day at a time when I could best benefit from their influence and input. This provided me an opportunity to *go to the mountain* so to speak and become immersed in and embraced by old time music on its home turf.

Even so, I was a link away from people such as Kyle Creed and his contemporaries. While most folks think I did okay, I still never got quite the experience or examples of those who went directly to visit them in person.

So, I came up with versions of many popular jam tunes be simple trial and error, using the available recordings including a good many jam tapes to guide my sound and the instruction of my local mentors — including Kevin Enoch, Mark Olitsky and Pete Smakula, then my boss — to guide my technique. Little did I know then how much I had changed and perhaps even missed.

The development of this book has shown me how much more I can still get out of these basic tunes and how much growth that still exists for me within the confines of what we have come to call *Old Time Music*. Through seeing and working with the transcriptions of Kyle's tunes and hearing his teaching where he breaks down what he plays (some examples accompany this book but for a more in depth listen, get Old Blue Records CD 502 - *Banjo Lessons on Kyle's Back Porch* - Kyle Creed and Tom Mylet) I have gained an entirely new insight into my playing that I would have never been aware of had it not been for the tabs presented here. For instance, you will notice that my versions don't tend to have either the dragged notes or galax lick and I don't use a pull off to an un-played string — techniques you will find often in Bob's transcriptions.

That said, in my *ignorance* of what Kyle did do, I found new or at least different ways to skin the same ... ah, banjo! Even Bob Carlin commented that he was surprised at how *Round Peak-ey* my versions sounded when he played out my transcriptions. So, we have included my more modern styled tabs of Kyle's playing in part to give you some more ideas to include in your variations of these tunes as well as show you how music—even *Old Time Music* is a fluid and living tradition which at both respects where it has come from while recognizing growth and development at the same time. It was Kyle himself who said, "you folks can do that if you like, but it just puts more work into it that way. ...But, you can do that if you want."

Don't worry if you don't play these tabs note for note as written. This music is to be enjoyed and interpreted through your hands as much as through ours. It is great to have the masters' guidance but in the end, you need to be true to yourself and enjoy the music. Just remember to ...

Play nice!

Dan Levenson, Yuma, AZ 2009

Big Liza Jane
as played by Kyle Creed

A part

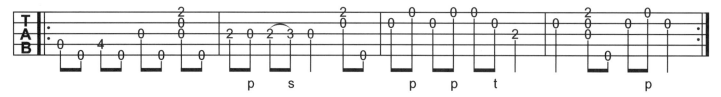

B part

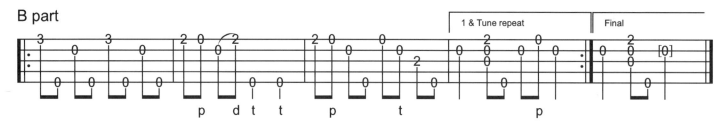

Alternate A measures 1 and 2

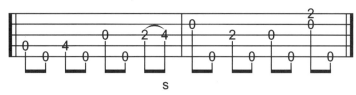

Kyle Creed on banjo and Roscoe Russell on guitar at Kyle's store outside of Galax, Virginia.

Big Liza Jane
as played by Dan Levenson

A part

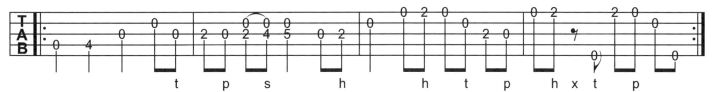

B part

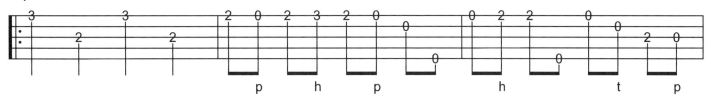

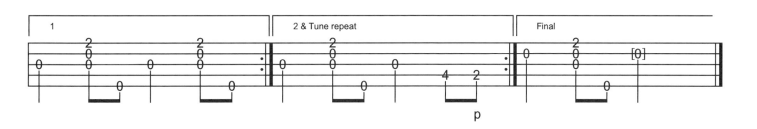

Alternate A measures 1 and 2

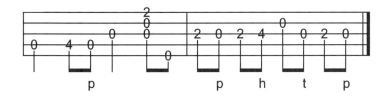

Black Eyed Susie
as played by Kyle Creed

A part

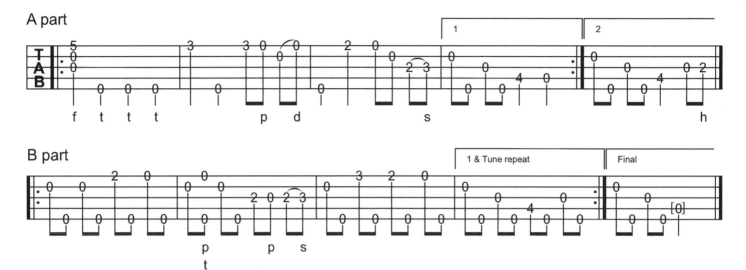

B part

The Camp Creek Boys as they appeared on the cover of their self-titled County LP, circa 1967
Standing left to right Fred Cockerham/fiddle, Kyle Creed/banjo and Ernest East/fiddle
Sitting Paul Sutphin/guitar, Verlin Clifton/mandolin and Ronald Collins/guitar

Black Eyed Susie

as played by Dan Levenson

A part

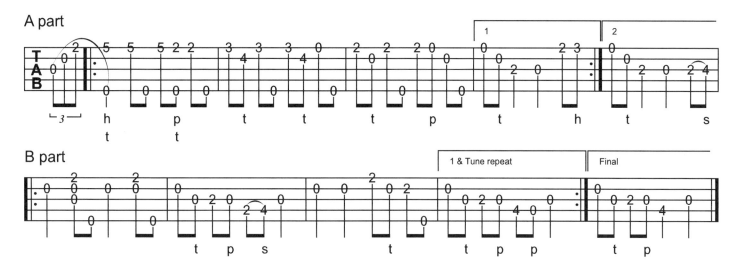

B part

Breaking Up Christmas
as played by Kyle Creed

A part

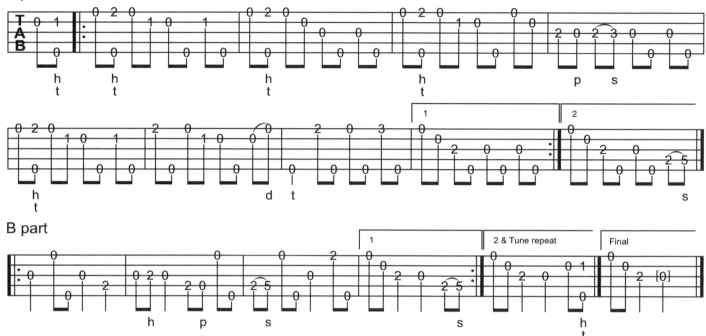

B part

Alternate B measures 1 and 2

Left to right: Bobby Patterson/guitar, Kyle Creed/fiddle
and Tom Norman/banjo.

Besides playing music with Kyle, Bobby founded Heritage Records, which bought the masters of Kyle's Mountain Records label and has been slowly reissuing them on CD including Creed's banjo recording, *Liberty*.

Tom Norman also played with fiddler Whit Sizemore in the Shady Mountain Ramblers.

Breaking Up Christmas

as played by Dan Levenson

A part

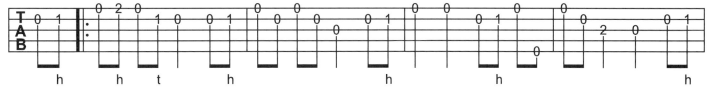

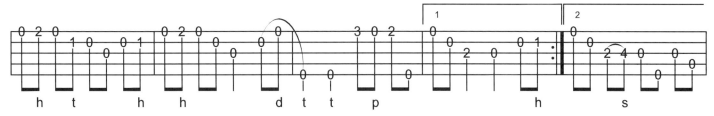

B part

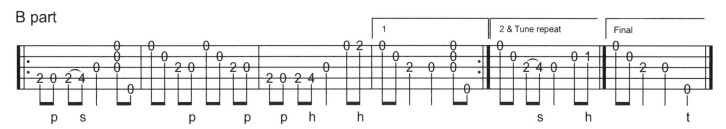

Alternate B measures 1 to 3

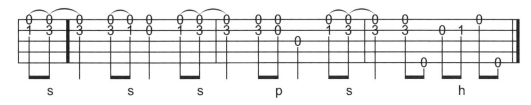

Buffalo Gals

as played by Kyle Creed

A tuning
aEAC#E (G capo 2)

A part

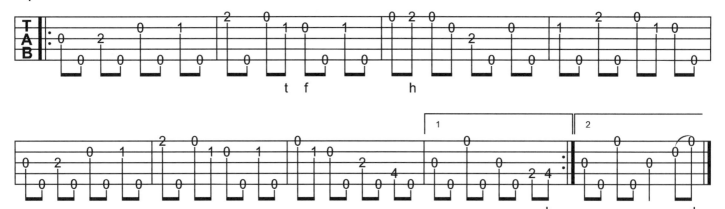

B part

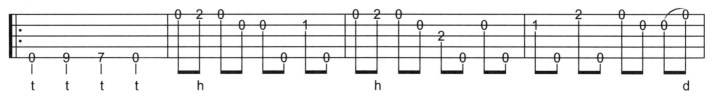

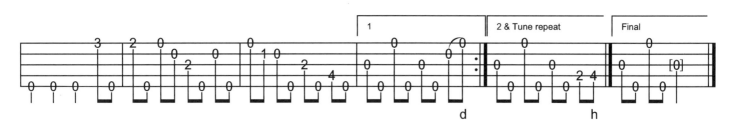

Alt measure A-7

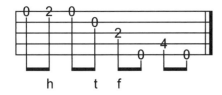

14

Buffalo Gals

as played by Dan Levenson

A part

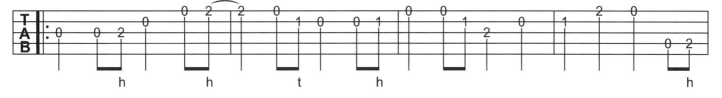

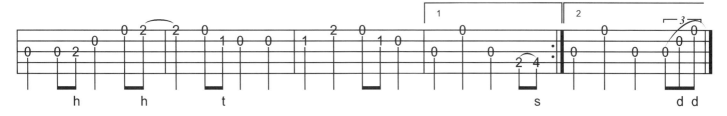

B part

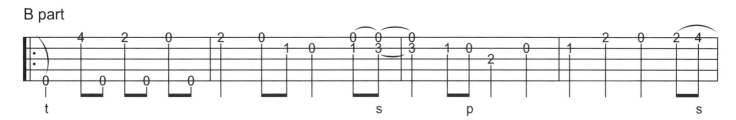

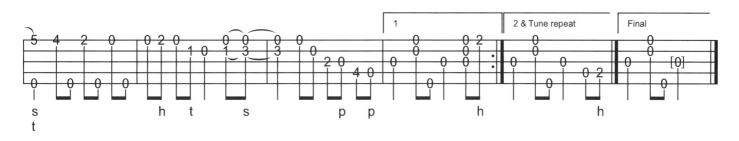

Cluck Old Hen

as played by Kyle Creed

A part

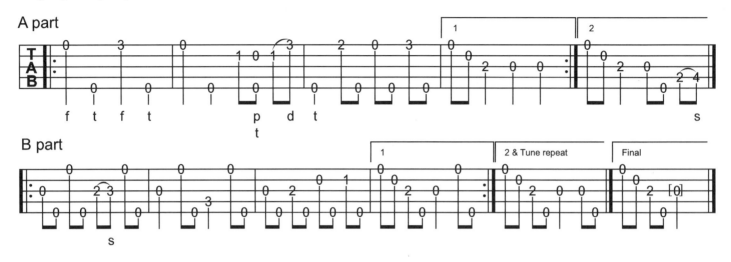

B part

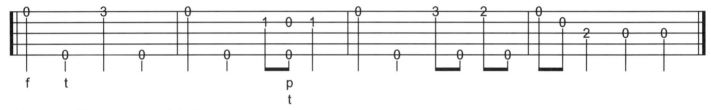

Alternate A part

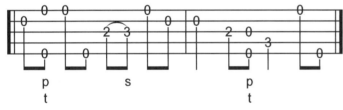

Alternate B measures 1 & 2

Kyle on banjo with Paul Sutphin on guitar
1967

16

Cluck Old Hen
as played by Dan Levenson

A part

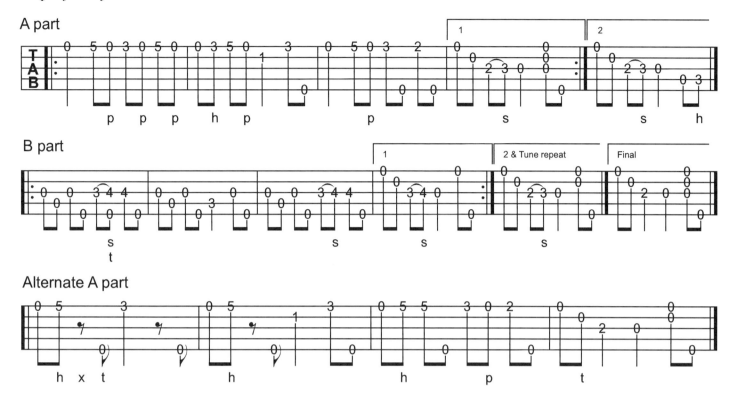

B part

Alternate A part

Alternate B measures 1 & 2

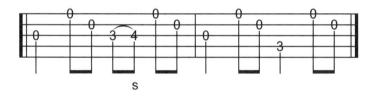

Cumberland Gap

as played by Kyle Creed

A part - x 3

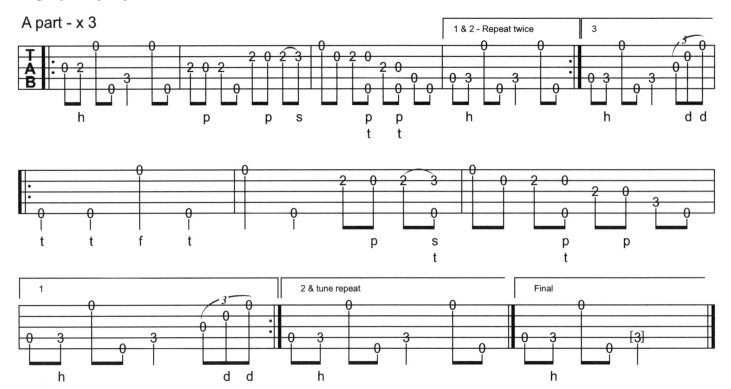

The best way to get into "Cumberland Gap" tuning is to start in the "G" tuning (gDGBD).
First, tune your fifth string down to match the first string noted at the fourth fret,
Next tune the second string noted at the fifth fret to the first string,
Then, the third string noted at the fifth fret to the second string and
Finally, the fourth string noted at the fifth fret to the third string.

This will get you into the "Cumberland Gap" tuning un-capoed.

Cumberland Gap
as played by Dan Levenson

Double D tuning
aDADE (double C capo 2)

A part - x 3

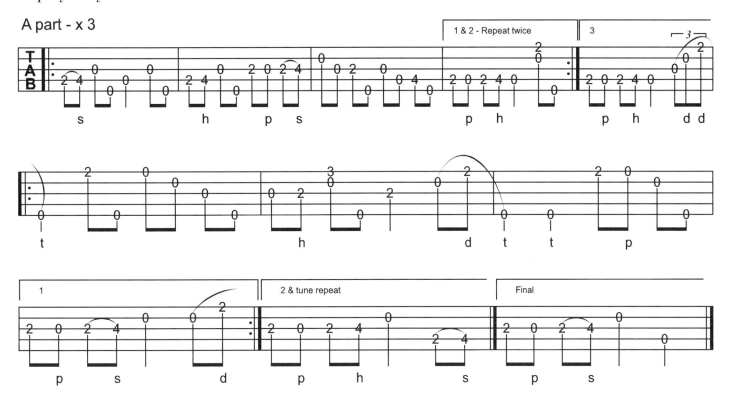

I don't use many tunings and prefer to play this one out of standard double D tuning. If you wanted this to be in E (like the Kyle version) then you could capo this to the 4th fret (second if you tune up) and then drop the fifth string down to the f#.

Darling Nellie Gray

as played by Kyle Creed

A part

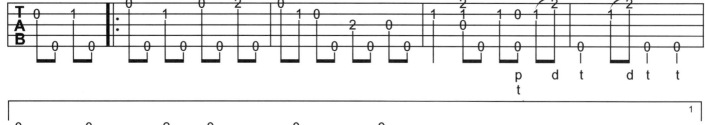

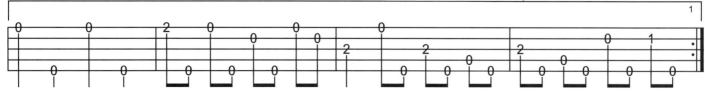

B part

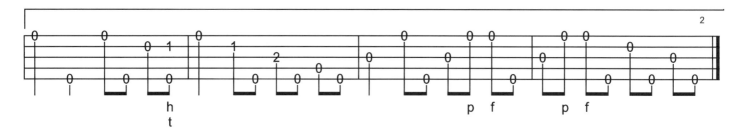

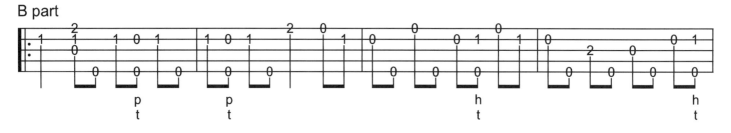

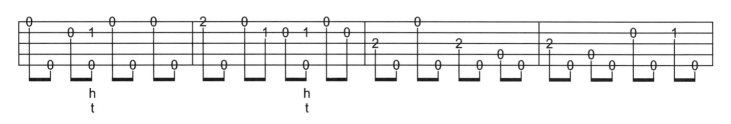

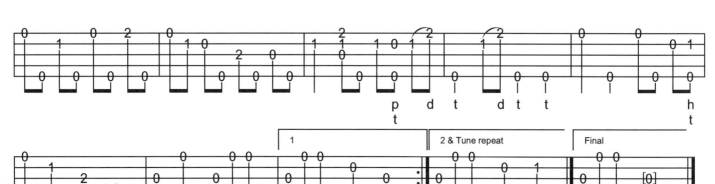

Darling Nellie Gray
as played by Dan Levenson

A tuning
aEAC#E (G capo 2)

A part

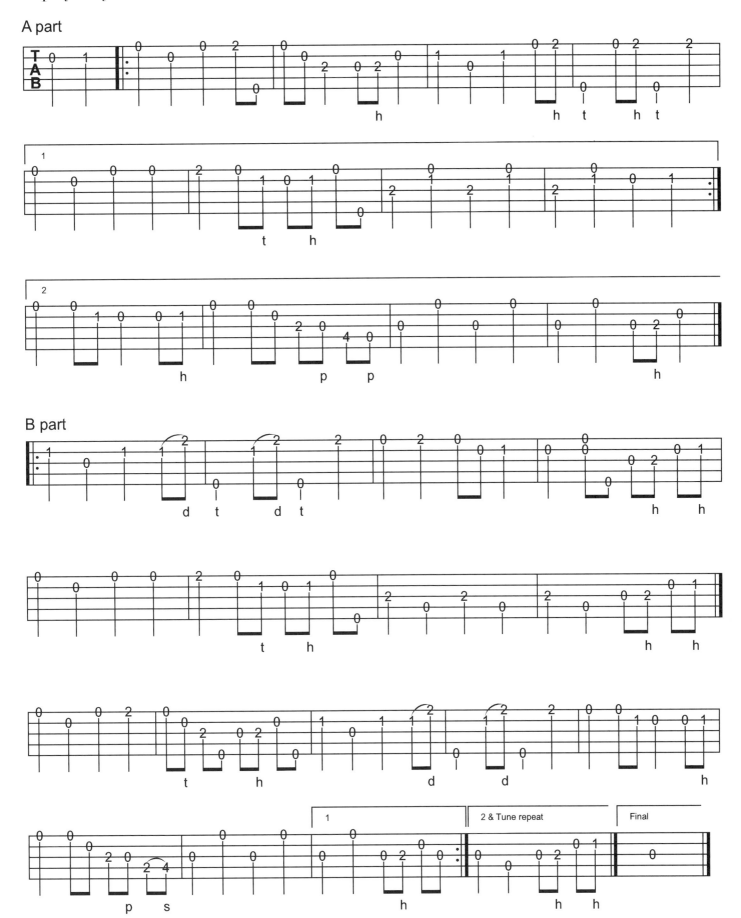

B part

Fall on My Knees

as played by Kyle Creed

Version 1

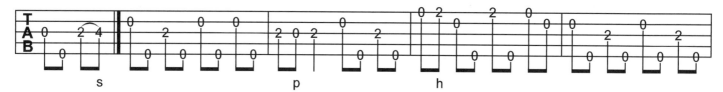

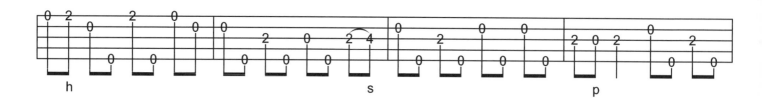

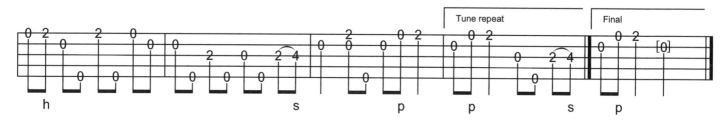

Version 2

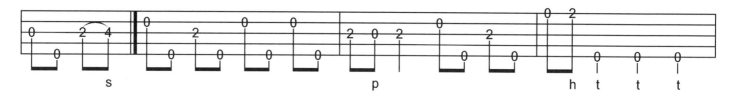

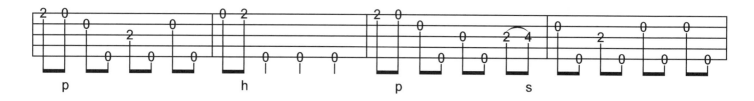

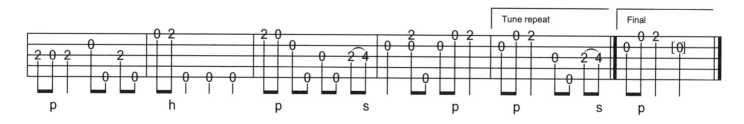

Alternate measure 3 of version 2

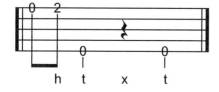

Fall on My Knees
as played by Dan Levenson

Version 1

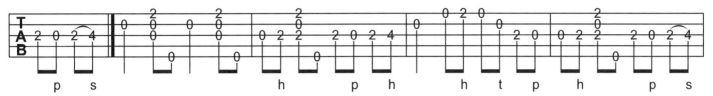

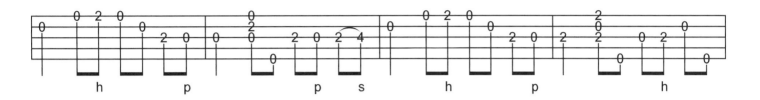

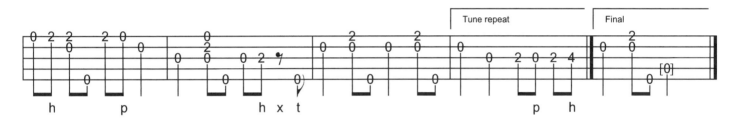

Version 2

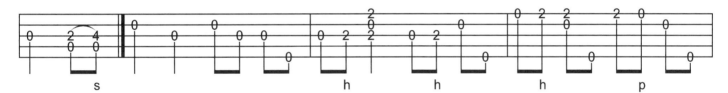

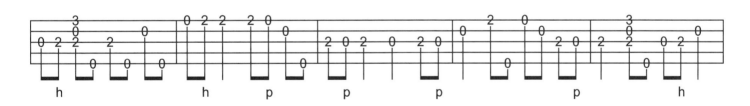

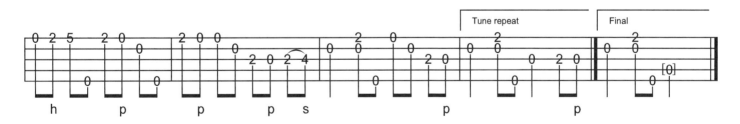

Fortune

as played by Kyle Creed

Double D tuning
aDADE (double C capo 2)

A part

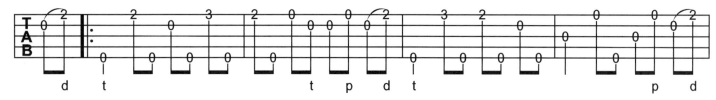

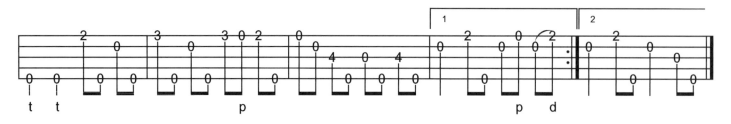

B part

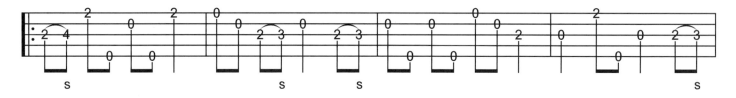

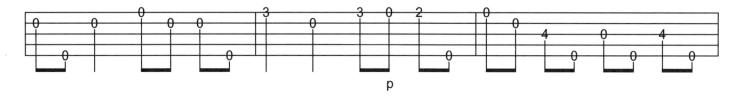

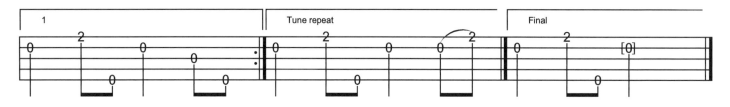

Fortune

as played by Dan Levenson

A part

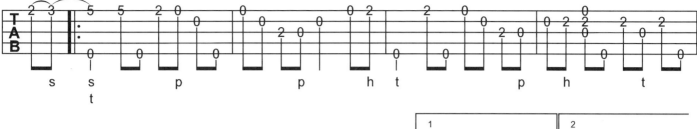

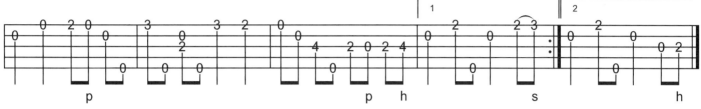

B part

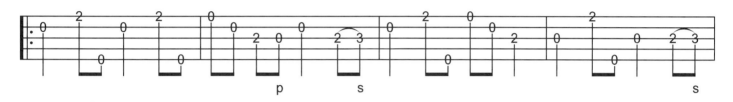

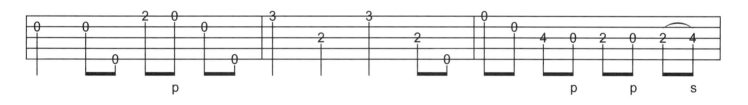

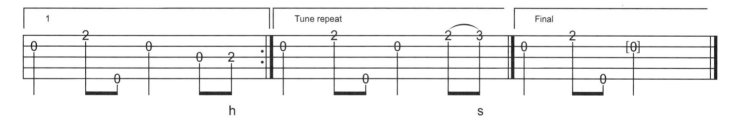

Jimmy Sutton

as played by Kyle Creed

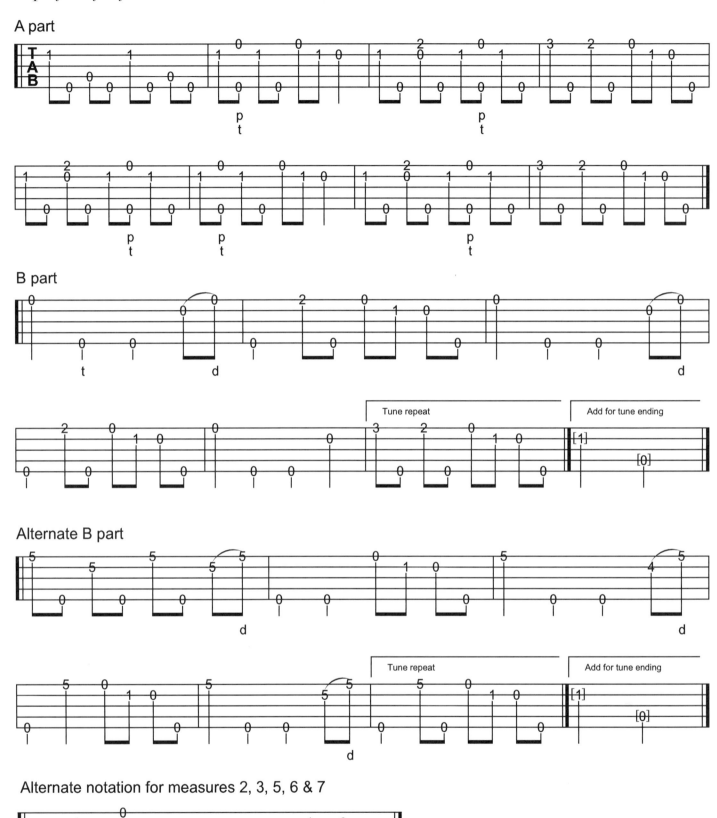

Alternate notation for measures 2, 3, 5, 6 & 7

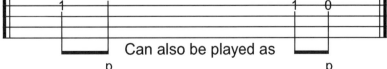

Can also be played as

Jimmy Sutton

as played by Dan Levenson

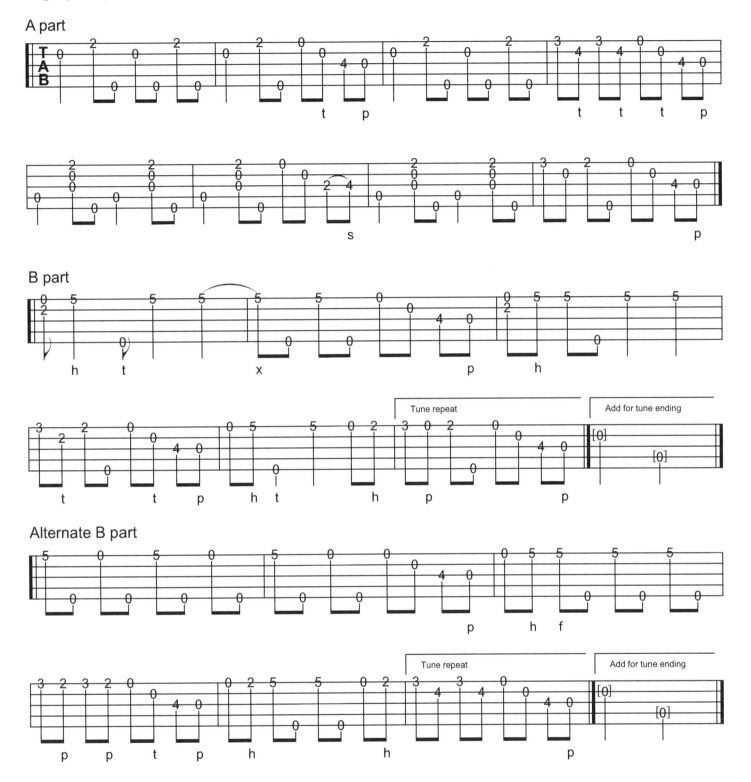

A part

B part

Alternate B part

Dan's note: I use regular double D tuning for this one as opposed to the tab of Kyle's playing which uses a second string dropped to a C#.

John Brown's Dream

as played by Kyle Creed

A part

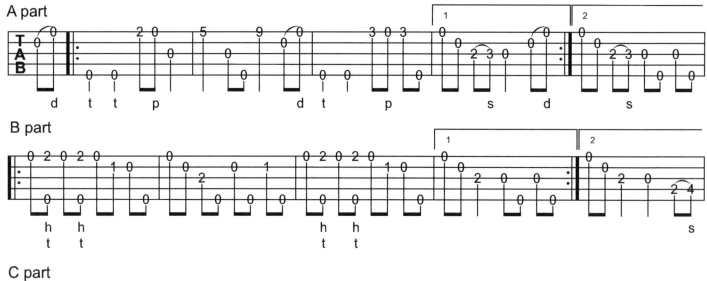

B part

C part

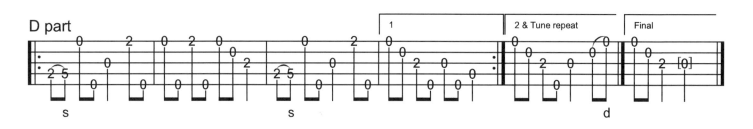

D part

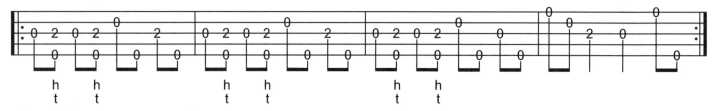

Alternate C part

A part alternate measure 2

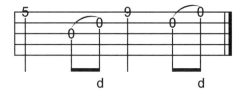

John Brown's Dream

as played by Dan Levenson

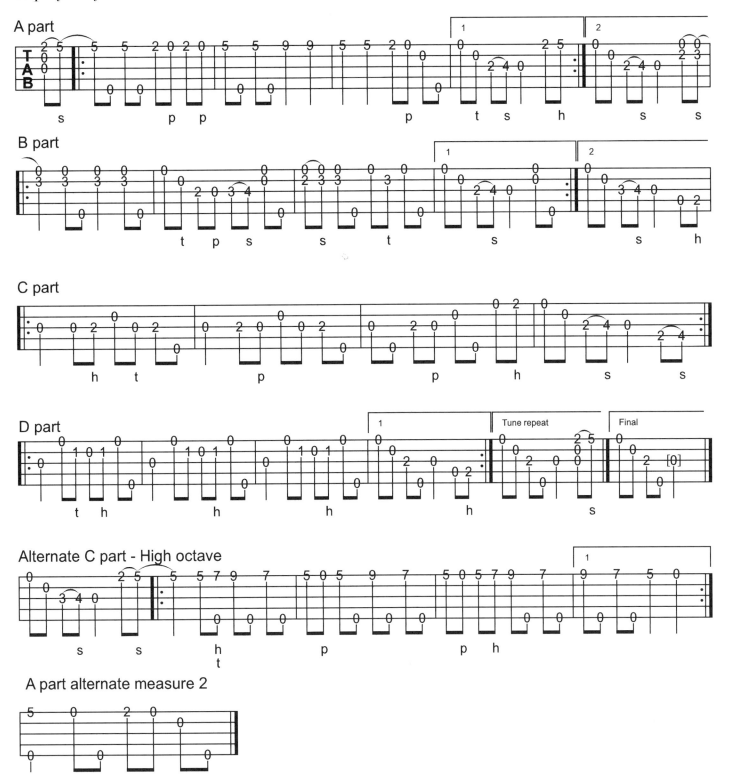

John Henry

as played by Kyle Creed

A part

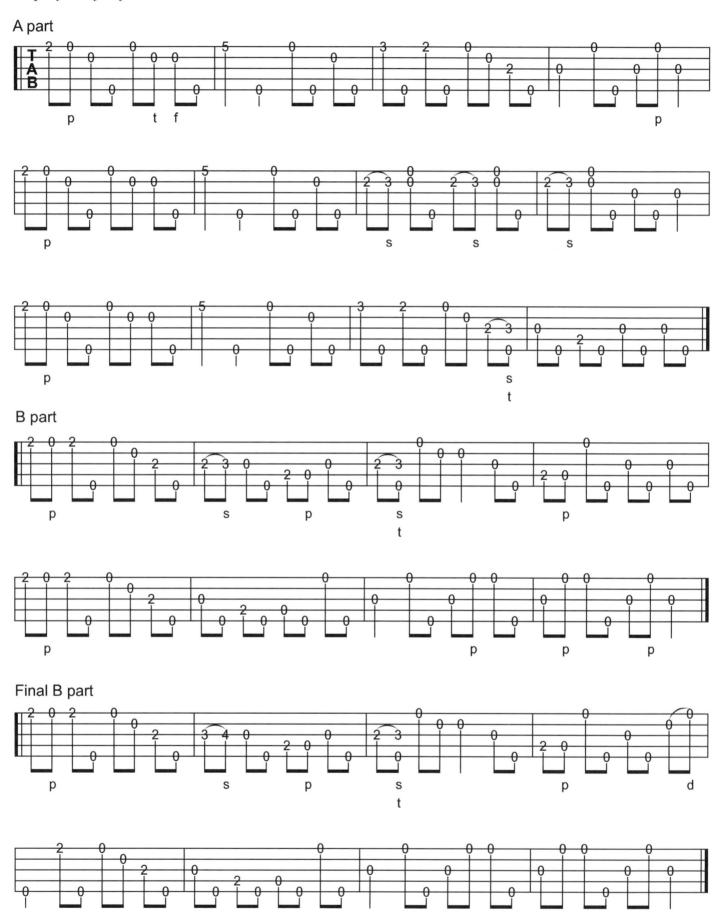

B part

Final B part

John Henry

as played by Dan Levenson

A part

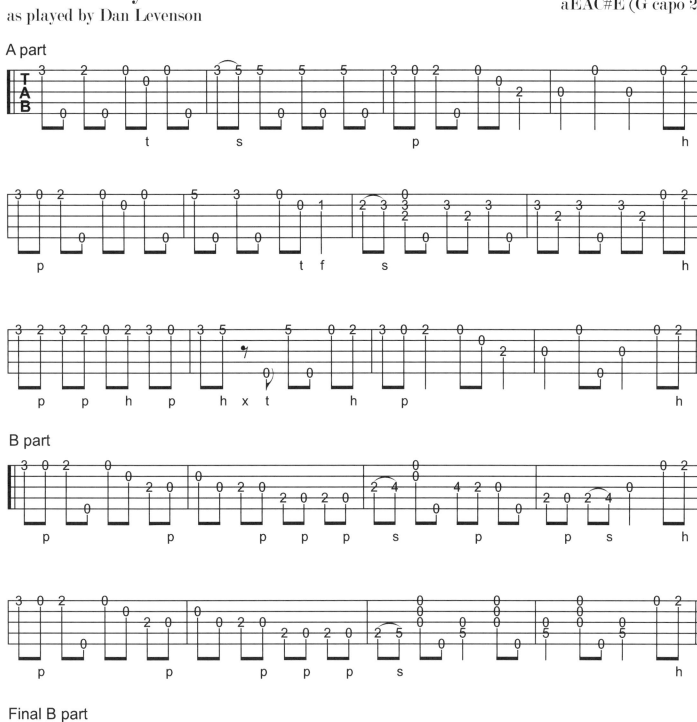

B part

Final B part

31

Katy Kline
as played by Kyle Creed

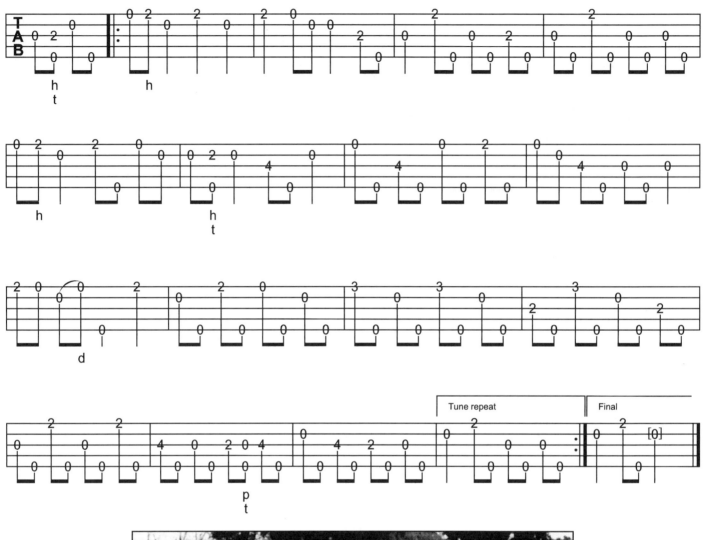

The Camp Creek Boys playing in Washington, DC
(Possibly at the Smithdonian Folklife Festival on the Mall)
Left to right is Ernest East/fiddle, Stella Kimble (another North Carolina musi-
cian), Kyle/banjo, unknown, Paul Sutphin/guitar and Verlin Clifton/mandolin

Katy Kline
as played by Dan Levenson

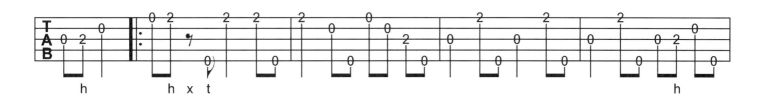

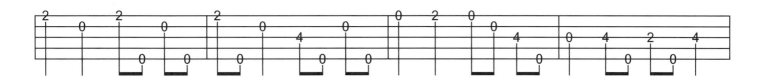

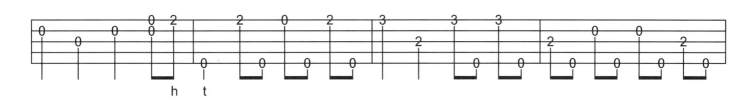

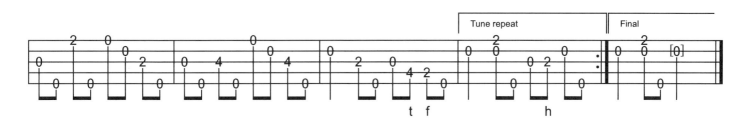

Little Liza Jane
as played by Kyle Creed

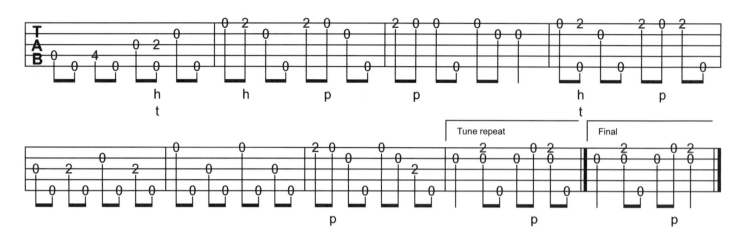

Alternate version

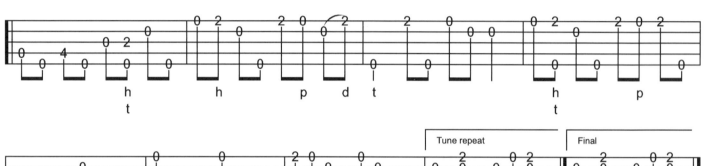

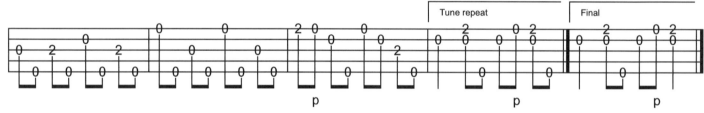

Little Liza Jane
as played by Dan Levenson

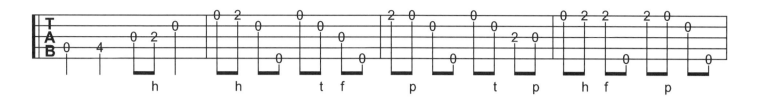

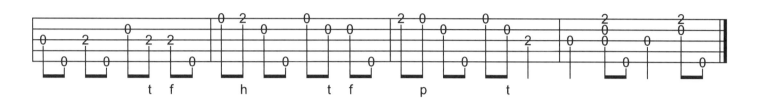

Mothman plays Banjo
Located in Point Pleasant, WV

Lost Indian
as played by Kyle Creed

A part

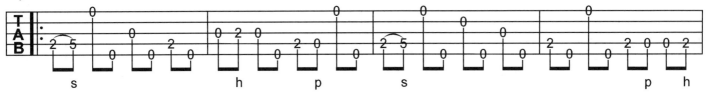

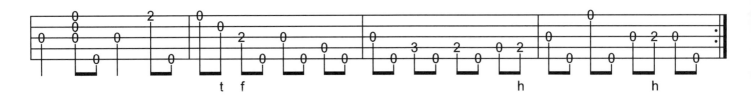

B part

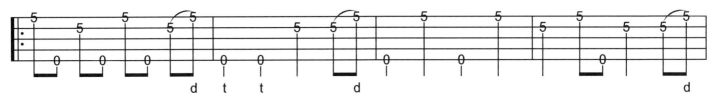

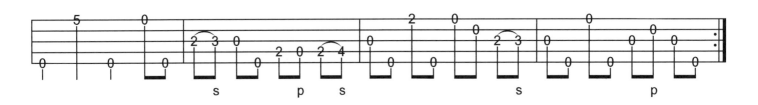

Notes: Kyle bars across the first and second strings at the fifth fret for the first half of the B part. The last measure of both the A and B parts are interchangeable variations. The only difference is the third beat, with the A using a hammer on and the B an open string pull off.

Lost Indian
as played by Dan Levenson

A part

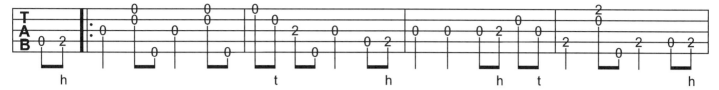

B part

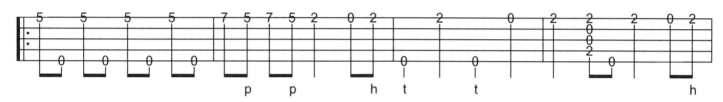

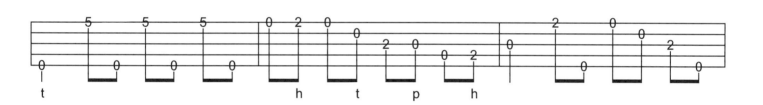

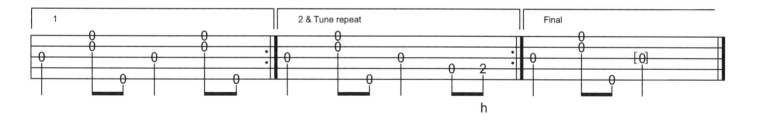

Mississippi Sawyer
as played by Kyle Creed

A part

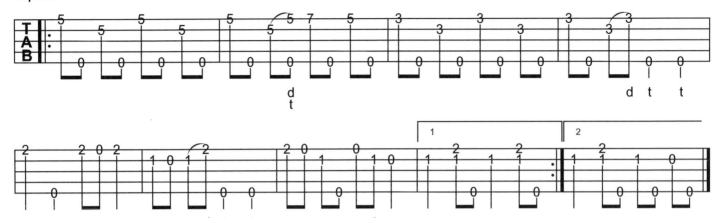

B part

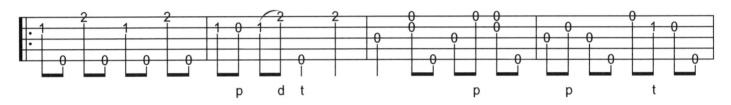

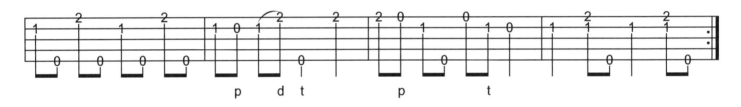

A part - Alternate 7th measure

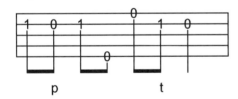

B part - Alternate 3rd and 4th measures

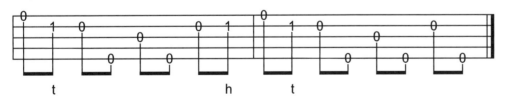

Mississippi Sawyer

as played by Dan Levenson

A part

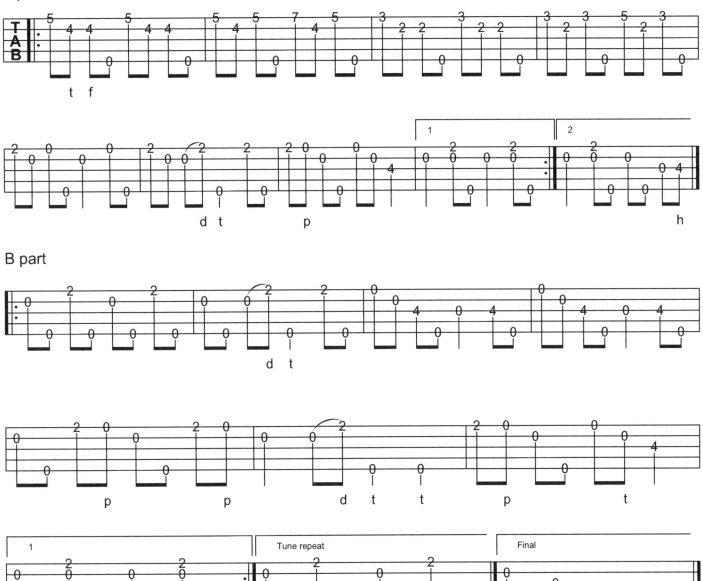

B part

Note: I use regular double D tuning for this one.

Old Molly Hare

as played by Kyle Creed

A part

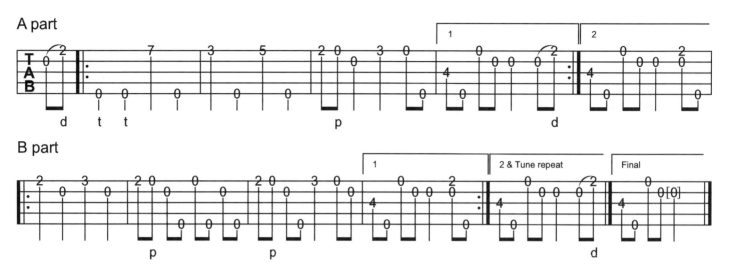

B part

Old Molly Hare
as played by Dan Levenson

Double D tuning
aDADE (double C capo 2)

A part

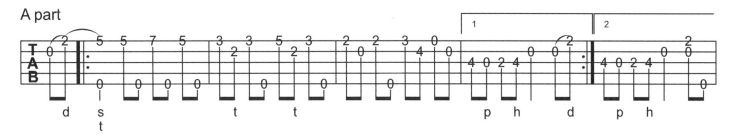

B part

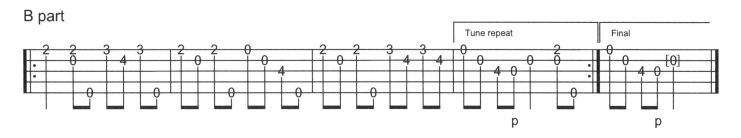

Dan's Southern Ohio homestead outside Gallipolis, OH

Polly Put the Kettle On

as played by Kyle Creed

Double D tuning
aDADE (double C capo 2)

A part

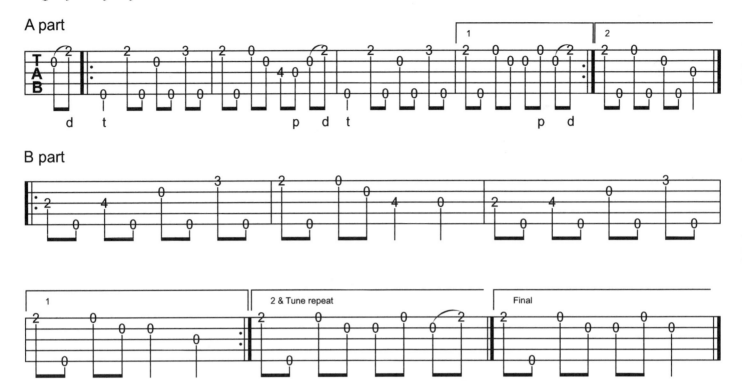

B part

Polly Put the Kettle On

as played by Dan Levenson

Double D tuning
aDADE (double C capo 2)

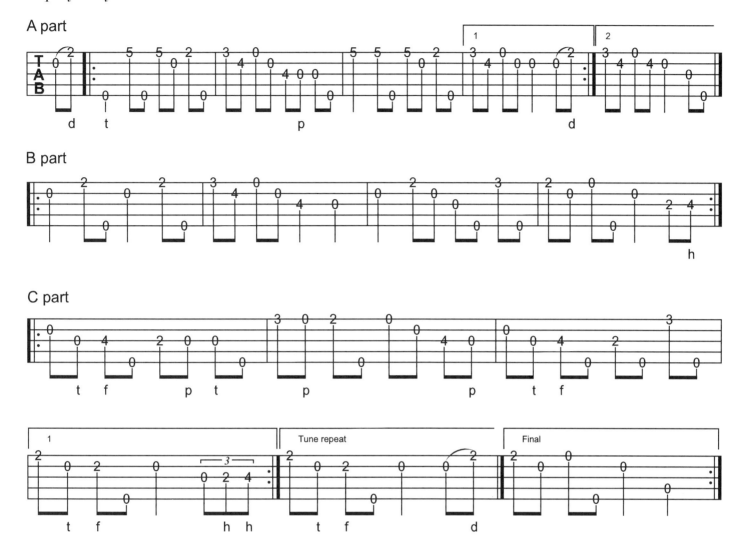

Dan's note: I use a third part which Kyle did not. If you wish to leave out that part, use my "Tune repeat" "Final" measures after the B part.

Pretty Little Girl

as played by Kyle Creed

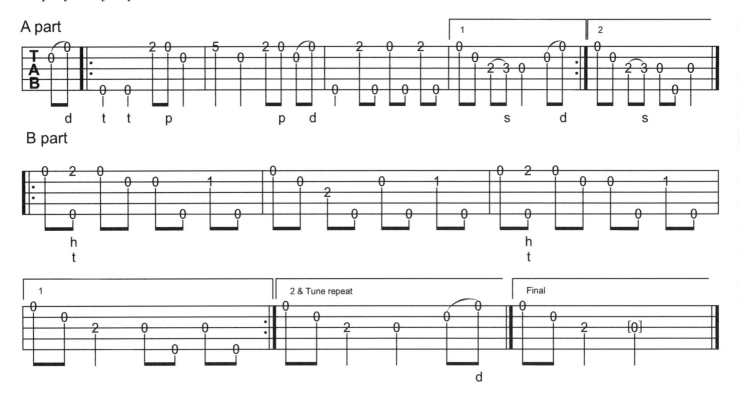

A small percentage of all the ribbons Kyle Creed
won over the years competing in area conventions.
Photo by Ken Landreth

Pretty Little Girl

as played by Dan Levenson

A tuning
aEAC#E (G capo 2)

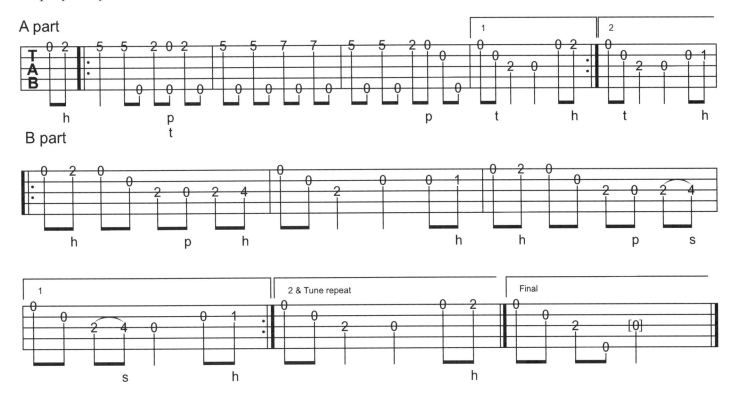

45

Rockingham Cindy

as played by Kyle Creed

Double D tuning
aDADE (double C capo 2)

A part

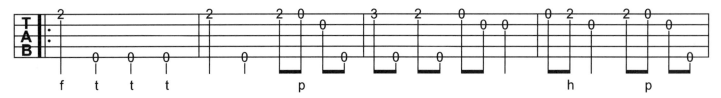

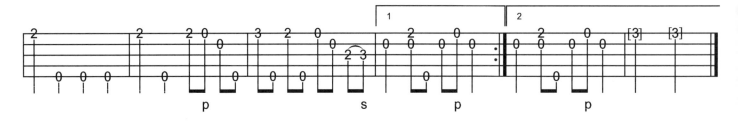

B part

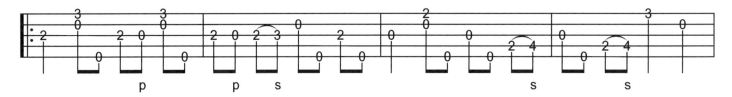

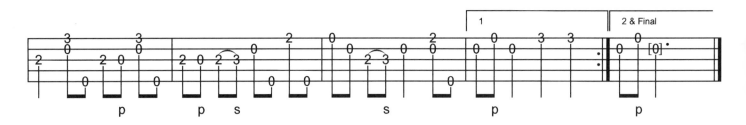

Alternate A measures 1-3

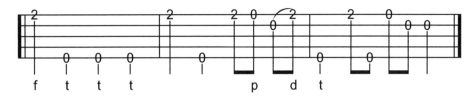

Rockingham Cindy

as played by Dan Levenson

A part

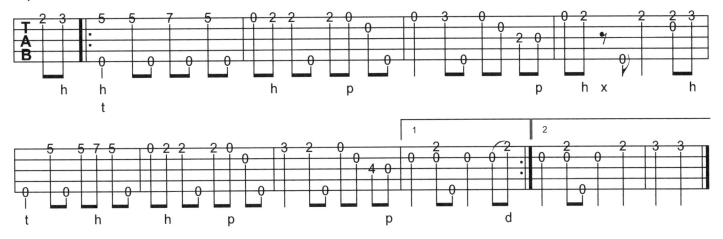

B part

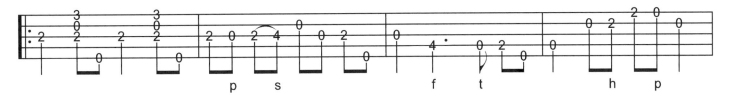

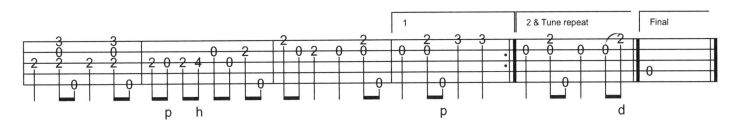

Roustabout

as played by Kyle Creed

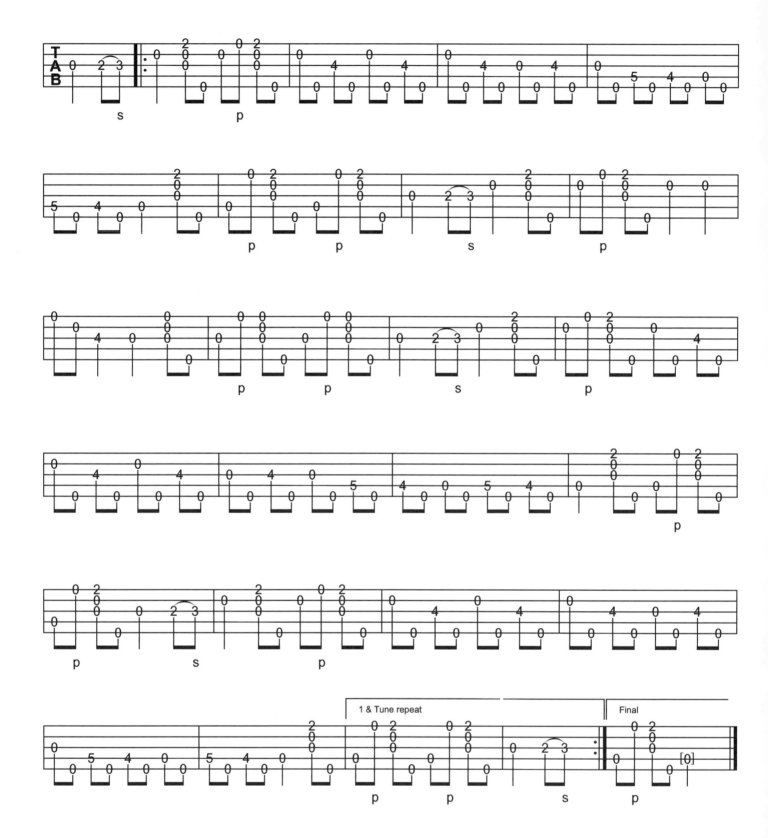

Roustabout

as played by Dan Levenson

Double D tuning
aDADE (double C capo 2)

Variant 1

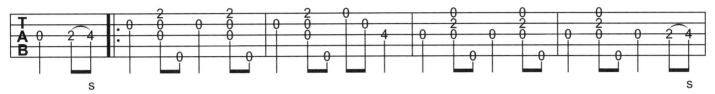

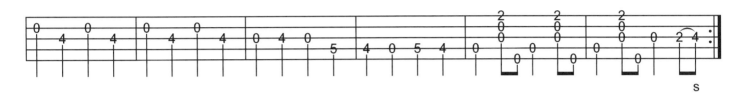

Variant 2

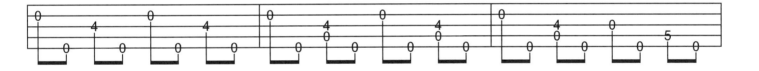

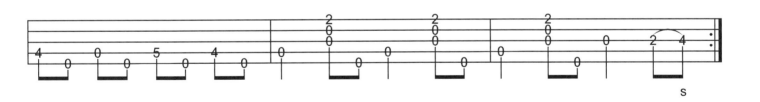

Dan's note: I don't see this tune so much a "tune" as a musical phrase that Kyle repeats and varies in how he plays it. I have tabbed what I feel to be the main "theme" of this tune in two ways. The second being much the same as the first except that the 5th measure and on is tabbed as all double thumb as Kyle often played AND with the added "bass" note which I just hear and feel the sound of both when I listen to it and play it myself.

I don't think you would want to try playing this one for any dances either.

Sail Away Ladies

As played by Kyle Creed

A part

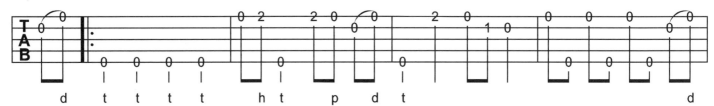

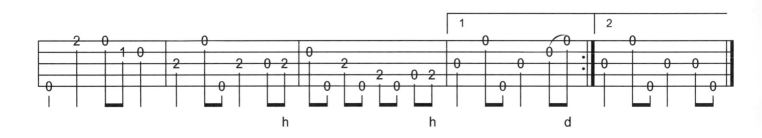

B part

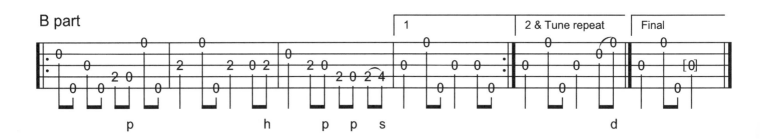

Tag 1 - Follows second B   (or) Tag 2

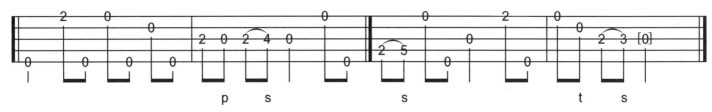

Alternate measure 1

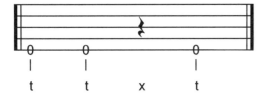

Sail Away Ladies

As played by Dan Levenson

A part

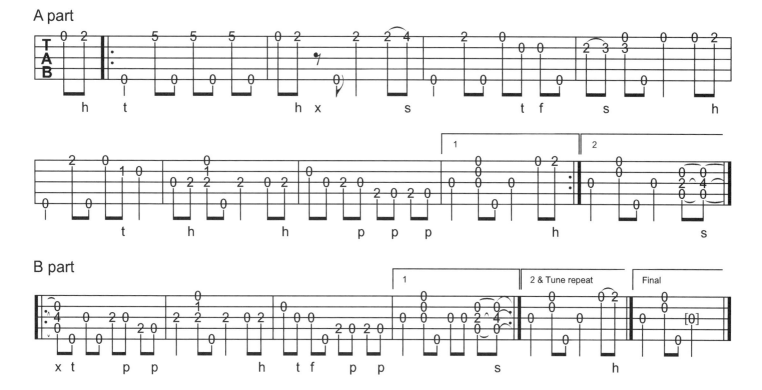

B part

Dan playing at Clifftop Stringband Festival, August 2000

Sally Ann - version 1

as played by Kyle Creed

Double D tuning
aDADE (double C capo 2)

A part

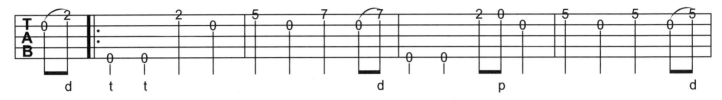

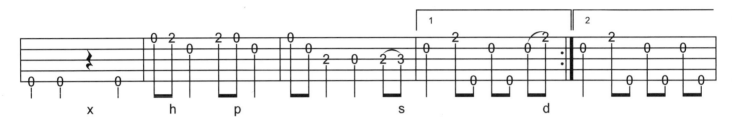

B part

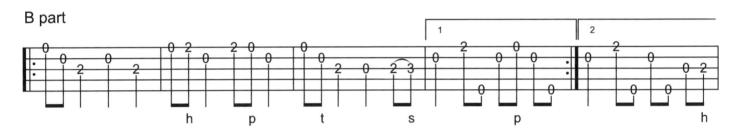

C part

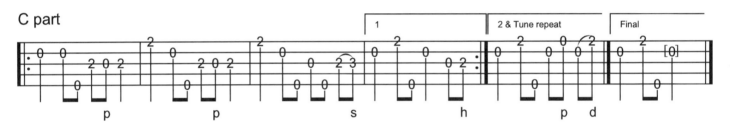

Alternate B part

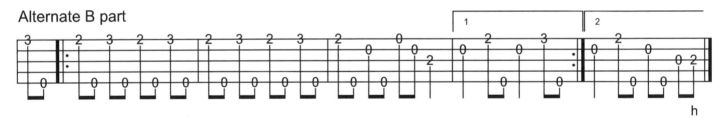

Sally Ann - version 1

as played by Dan Levenson

Double D tuning
aDADE (double C capo 2)

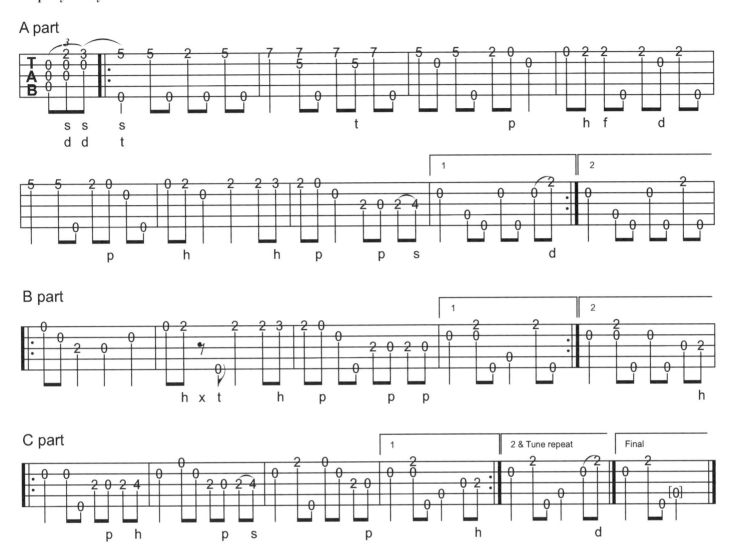

Sally Ann - version 2

as played by Kyle Creed

Double D tuning
aDADE (double C capo 2)

A part

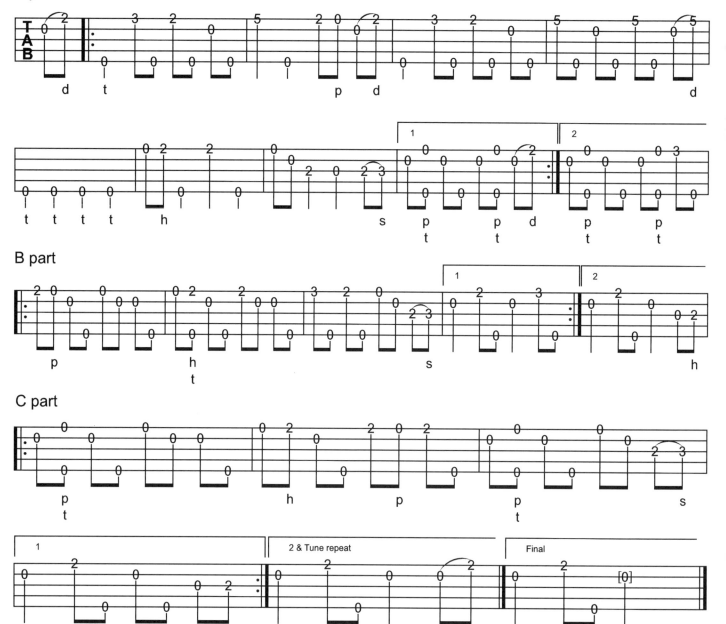

B part

C part

A Biography of Kyle Creed

Andy Kyle Robert Creed (September 20, 1912-November 26, 1982) was born in the mountain community of Low Gap, in North Carolina's Surry County. Kyle's grandfather, Bob Creed, was a fiddler, as was his father Qualey. His Uncle John Lowe was a prime influence on Kyle's clawhammer banjo style. As Kyle said: "I've got exactly the lick he's got. You know, sometimes people will double a string; now he'll do it, and I do. For instance there's sometimes where I'll hit a string twice, where most'll hit it once. . . . Well, when I was growing up I stayed at his house in northern Virginia, in Winchester, for one winter working in apples up there. . . . Had a session about every night; that's what teaches you, you know; you pick a tune and then come in next night and pick the same tune again."

Once reaching adulthood, Kyle worked primarily in construction, often moving far from his home in the Blue Ridge. When Creed settled outside of Galax, Virginia, Kyle became reacquainted with musicians such as Fred Cockerham, Tommy Jarrell, Ernest East and their ilk. He joined in to make some of the most memorable of the "Round Peak" music in a period that coincided with the discovery by outsiders of the persuasive old time music being made in the region.

His prominence on *Clawhammer Banjo* and *The Camp Creek Boys* sessions made by Charlie Faurot and issued on County Records, along with Tommy Jarrell's *June Apple* and Kyle's banjo album *Liberty*, insured that Creed would enter the banjo pantheon for younger players. And it didn't hurt Kyle's business that he used banjos of his own making for those recordings and that Creed was pictured holding those distinctive looking instruments on their album covers.

Kyle Creed was also a mainstay at area fiddlers' conventions, at first backing prominent fiddlers such as Fred Cockerham and Ernest East in the Camp Creek Boys, and later leading his own band on the fiddle. To add to the impact created by his appearances on albums for County Records, Kyle also participated in the early Brandywine Mountain Music Conventions, giving northern musicians their first exposure to the Round Peak sound.

Although Kyle Creed may have made a banjo as a teenager (probably for his own use), most of his instruments date from the period after Creed returned to the Blue Ridge Mountains in the early 1960s through his death in 1982.

Kyle purchased a store from the Melton family that became his shop, recording studio and record label headquarters and home around 1961 or 1962. He then associated himself with blacksmith and barber Pearly Bryant (1903-1972), who made a small number of banjos from the 1940s until the 1970s. Pearly undoubtedly passed along to Kyle much of his knowledge about banjos, as Bryant made the majority of his parts and even cast his own tone rings. In total, there could be as many as 200 Kyle Creed necks or whole banjos in existence based on those with serial numbers and what Kyle told those who knew him.

Kyle Creed banjos have a distinctive sound—bassy and a bit muffled but big and percussive—that is best heard in Kyle's own banjo playing. In fact, Creed liked to "test drive" every instrument he made, playing the first tune on them and keeping them around as his primary player until the banjo was sold. He also used a homemade fingerpick (from a brass Buick headlight holder) on his frailing finger to give his melody notes a clarity and attack.

Kyle muted his fifth string, probably because of his constant use of the string as every other note.

Step Back Cindy

as played by Kyle Creed

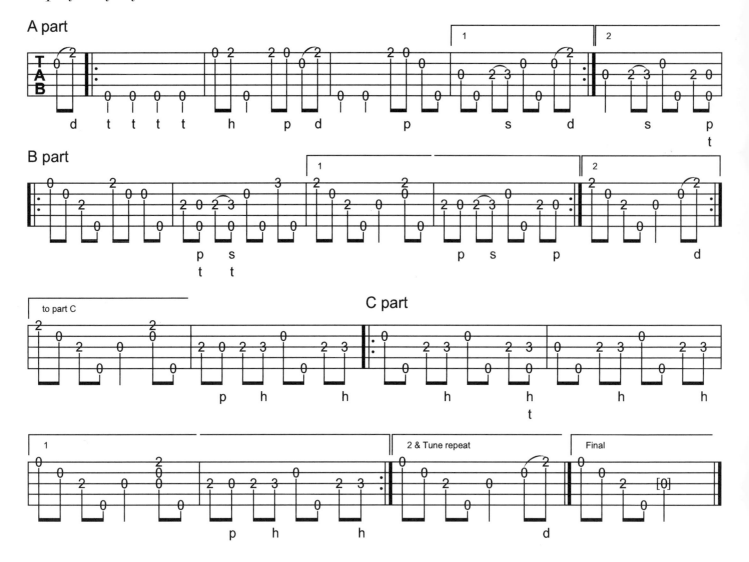

Play this AA BB AA BB CC

Step Back Cindy
as played by Dan Levenson

Double D tuning
aDADE (double C capo 2)

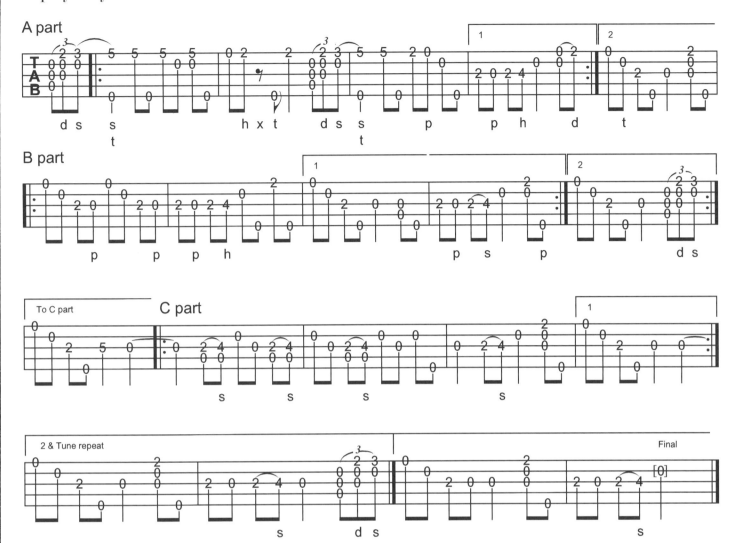

You are going to find a LOT of variations on this one.

As written here you play this AA BB AA B CC

Note, that when going to the C part from the B part, you skip both the 1st and 2nd endings. Yes, you use the "To C part" measure there.

Stillhouse

as played by Kyle Creed

Double D tuning
aDADE (double C capo 2)

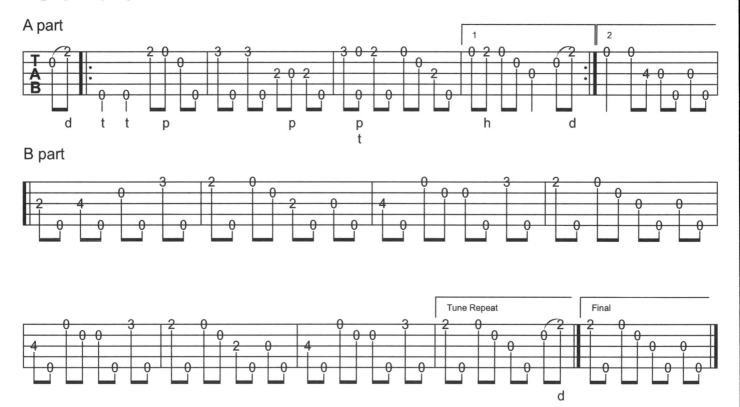

Photographs of Kyle Creed surrounded by his
personal instrument & banjo case.
On the left is the first banjo he ever made.
The Kyle Creed Banjo Show, Galax, VA,
September 12, 2009. Photo by Ken Landreth

Stillhouse

as played by Dan Levenson

Double D tuning
aDADE (double C capo 2)

A part

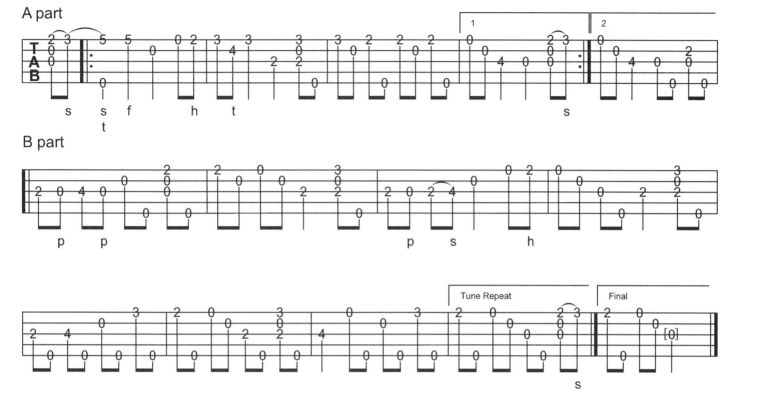

B part

Banjo and fiddle at Dan's homestead outside
Gallipolis, Ohio

Sugar Hill

as played by Kyle Creed

Double D tuning
aDADE (double C capo 2)

A part

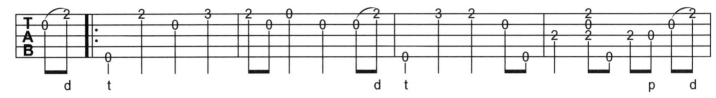

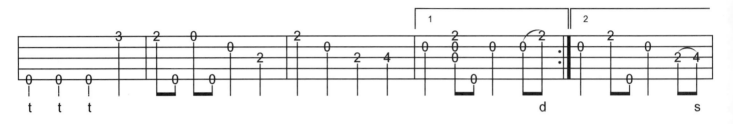

B part

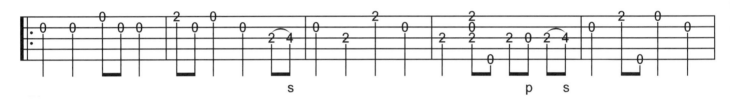

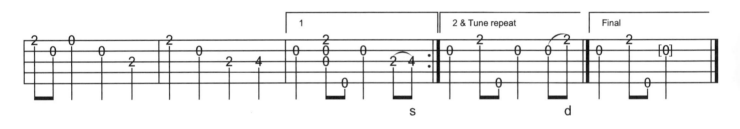

Sugar Hill

as played by Dan Levenson

Double D tuning
aDADE (double C capo 2)

A part

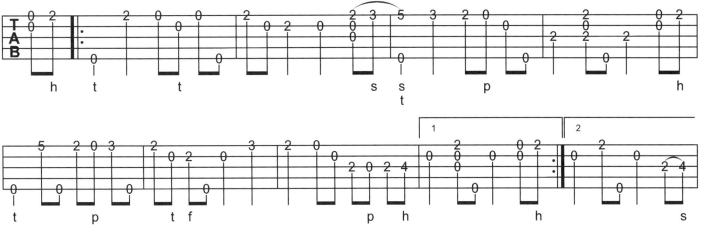

B part

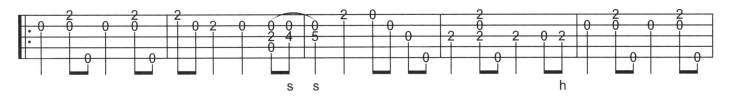

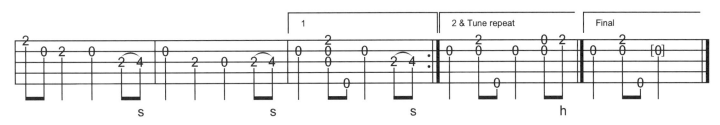

Dan's note: I usually play this tune with the noted "B" part as the first part since it would be the verse. I have written it with the parts noted the same way as Kyle played it to avoid confusion.

Also, for some reason you will notice that I often use the second finger on the second fret of the second string instead of the open first string. There is no real reason and you could substitute the open first if you prefer.

Western Country (aka Suzannah Gal)

as played by Kyle Creed

Double D tuning
aDADE (double C capo 2)

A part

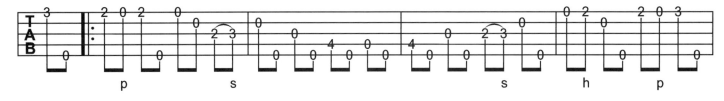

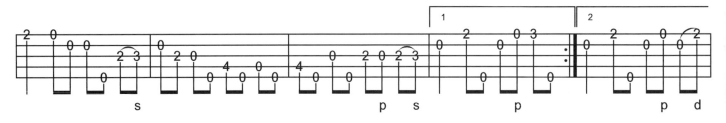

B part

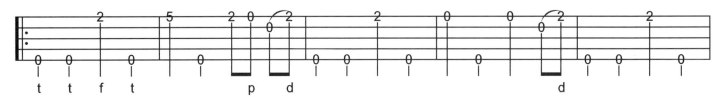

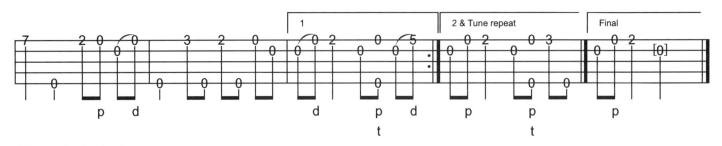

Alternate A start

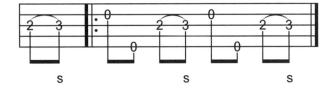

Western Country (aka Suzannah Gal)

as played by Dan Levenson

Double D tuning
aDADE (double C capo 2)

A part

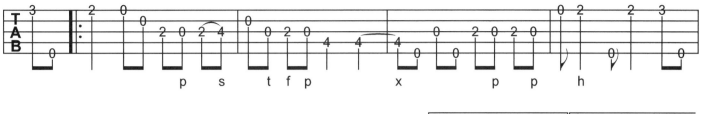

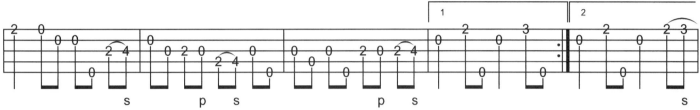

B part

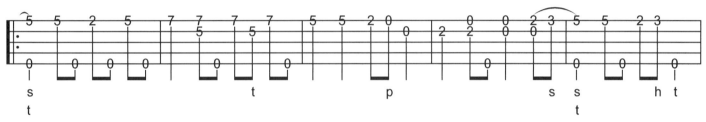

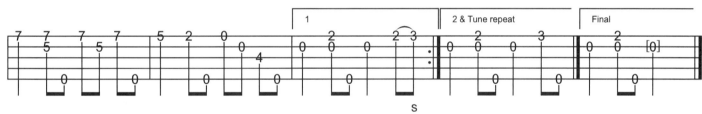

Alternate A start

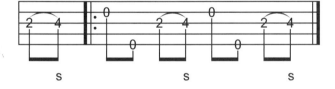

63

Dan Levenson is a Southern Appalachian native who has grown up with the music of the region. Today he is considered to be a master teacher and performer of both the Clawhammer banjo & Appalachian fiddle style.

Dan has won many awards on both instruments including first place at the 2005 Ohio Clawhammer Banjo Championship and Grand Champion at the 2010 Ajo, AZ fiddle contest. He has over 10 recordings both with his band The Boiled Buzzards and in solo configurations. Dan teaches regularly throughout the country and has taught at many of the traditional music schools and camps including the John C. Campbell Folk School, Mars Hill, Maryland Banjo Academy, the St. Louis Folk School, The Rocky Mountain Fiddle Camp and Banjo Camp North. He currently also runs various clawhammer banjo workshops as well as his innovative *Clawcamp* throughout the year.

Dan is the Mel Bay author of *Clawhammer Banjo From Scratch, Buzzard Banjo Clawhammer Style, Old Time Festival Tunes for Clawhammer Banjo,* and *Gospel Tunes for Clawhammer Banjo.* He is a writer for *The Old Time Herald* as well as a writer and editor for *Banjo Newsletter's Old Time Way.*

For Dan's other books and recordings and more information about Dan, please go to
www.Clawdan.com

Bob Carlin is probably the best known clawhammer style banjoist performing today. Faithful to timeless Southern Traditions, he has taken the distinctive southern banjo style to appreciative audiences all over the US, Canada, Europe, Australia and Japan. As a solo performer, and a member of John Hartford's Stringband, Bob has appeared at countless festivals, clubs, schools and museums. Carlin is a three-time winner of the Frets Magazine reader's poll, and has four Rounder albums to his credit.

Marty Stuart, organizer Trish Kilby Fore and author Bob Carlin at the Kyle Creed Banjo Show. Marty has a real Creed "checkerboard" and Bob holds Kevin Fore's takeoff on the same style Kyle. Photo by Ken Landreth.

Bob Carlin has studied both in person and on transcriptions the work of master players from previous generations. Along with researching several books and countless articles, this has made Carlin one of the foremost experts on the history of the banjo and its playing styles. Bob has authored several instruction manuals and six DVDs on how to play clawhammer banjo. This has all combined to make Bob Carlin one of the most in-demand teachers at camps, workshops and festivals.

For Bob's other books and recordings and more information about Bob, please go to
www.bobcarlinmusic.com